Alfred's Premier Piano Course

Dennis Alexander • Gayle Kowalchyk • E. L. Lancaster • Victoria McArthur • Martha Mier

Theory Book 3 is designed to correlate with Lesson and Performance Books 3 of *Alfred's Premier Piano Course*. When used together, they offer a fully integrated and unparalleled comprehensive approach to piano instruction.

In addition to written theory, unique features of the book include:

- *Fun Zone*—Explore music through written games and puzzles that truly make theory fun!

- *Imagination Station*—Learn to compose and create.

- *Learning Link*—Discover facts related to history, science, and interesting subjects from daily life based on the music and activities in the course.

- *Now Hear This*—Learn how to listen to music through ear training. Most of these exercises should be done in the lesson.

- *Now Play This*—Learn to sight-read music.

The pages in this book are correlated page by page with the material in Lesson Book 3. They should be assigned according to the instructions in the upper right corner of each page of this book. They may be assigned as review material at any time after the student has passed the designated Lesson Book page.

Edited by Morton Manus

Cover Design by Ted Engelbart
Interior Design by Tom Gerou
Illustrations by Jimmy Holder
Music Engraving by Linda Lusk

Copyright © MMVII by Alfred Publishing Co., Inc.
All Rights Reserved.   Printed in USA.
ISBN-10: 0-7390-4750-7
ISBN-13: 978-0-7390-4750-7

Just turn the page to start your exploration of the fascinating world of music theory!

Use with Alfred's Premier Piano Course,
Lesson Book Level 3, pages 2–3.

Fun Zone   Sailing the Nile River

Follow the directions as you visit the sights in Egypt while sailing on the world's longest river. *Begin at the bottom of the page.*

Learning Link

The **Nile River** flows north from Sudan, through Egypt, to the Mediterranean Sea.

1. **Abu Simbel** is a set of two temples built for Ramesses II, a pharaoh who ruled in the 13th century.

2. The **Aswan High Dam** was completed in 1960 to control flooding of the Nile.

3. The **Temple of Karnak** is the largest temple in Egypt and took 1,300 years to build.

4. The **Valley of the Kings** contains many tombs of ancient pharaohs.

5. The **Pyramids of Giza** include 3 pyramids. They are one of the Seven Wonders of the Ancient World.

6. **Alexandria** is a port city and was home to another Ancient Wonder, the Lighthouse of Alexandria, that was probably destroyed in an earthquake.

6. With your RH, play a G major scale.

Alexandria

5. Write the interval name, then play.

Pyramids of Giza

Valley of the Kings

4. With your LH, play a C major scale.

3. Name the chords (**I** or **V⁷**), then play.

Temple of Karnak

2. Write the interval name, then play.

Aswan High Dam

Abu Simbel

1. Name the chords (**I** or **V⁷**), then play.

Begin here

1. Now Play This: Play and count aloud.

2. Now Hear This: Circle the pattern that your teacher plays.*

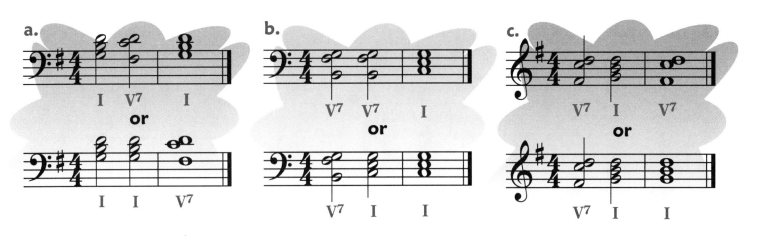

Imagination Station

*Using this rhythm, create a RH melody with notes
chosen from the G major scale. Begin and end with G.*

*Note to Teacher: Play one pattern from each exercise.

4

The IV Chord in C

1. The names of the notes in the **I** chord in C are:

C E A
B E G
C E G

(circle one set)

2. The names of the notes in the **IV** chord in C are:

C F G
C F A
C E A

(circle one set)

3. To move from the **I** chord to the **IV** chord:

raise
lower   the middle note a   half
whole   step.

(circle one)   *(circle one)*

raise
lower   the top note a   half
whole   step.

(circle one)   *(circle one)*

4. Write **I**, **IV** or **V⁷** on each blank line. Then play and count aloud.

The IV Chord in G

1. The names of the notes in the **I** chord in G are:

G A D
G B D
G C D

(circle one set)

2. The names of the notes in the **IV** chord in G are:

G C D
G B E
G C E

(circle one set)

3. Circle the Roman numerals that match the chord pattern on the staff. Then play the chords.

a.

IV I V⁷ I
or
IV I IV I

b.

IV IV I
or
IV I I

c.

I V⁷ I
or
I IV I

4. **Now Hear This:** Circle the pattern that your teacher plays.*

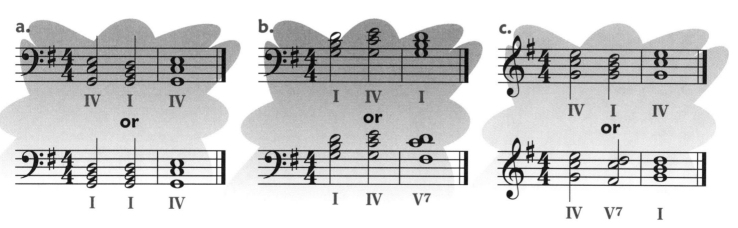

a.
IV I IV
or
I I IV

b.
I IV I
or
I IV V⁷

c.
IV I IV
or
IV V⁷ I

***Note to Teacher:** Play one pattern from each exercise.

6

Fun Zone Getting Directions

1. **Composer Quest** You have found directions to Wolfgang Amadeus Mozart's house on the Internet. Trace your route on the map by following the directions below.

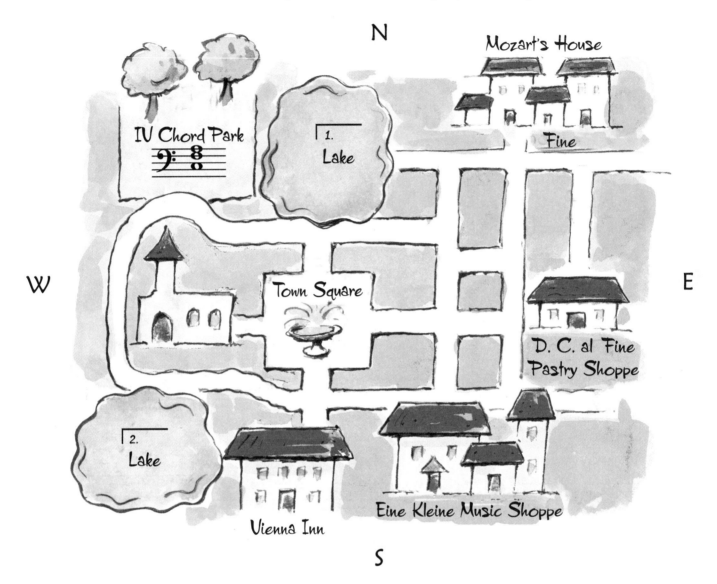

a. Begin at the **Vienna Inn.**

b. Go N through the **Town Square.**

c. Continue N to **First Ending Lake.**

d. Go W to **IV Chord Park.**

e. Go S to **Second Ending Lake.**

f. Go E to the **Eine Kleine Music Shoppe.**

g. Go N to the **Fine** at **Mozart's House.**

2. **D. C.** means repeat from the | beginning / previous measure

(circle one)

3. **Fine** means | beginning / end

4. **D. C. al Fine** is a(n) | French / Italian | term.

5. When you play the 2nd ending, you | repeat / skip | the 1st ending.

Imagination Station

*You are invited to play at Carnegie Hall! Get ready by writing **I**, **IV** or **V⁷** on the blank line for the correct LH chord in each measure. Then play and count aloud.*

Tips for Choosing the Correct Chord

Use **I** when most of the melody notes in the measure are 1-3-5 of the scale:

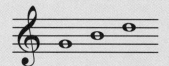

Use **V⁷** when most of the melody notes in the measure are 2-4-5 of the scale:

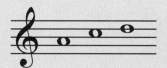

Use **IV** when most of the melody notes in the measure are 1-4-6 of the scale:

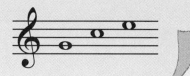

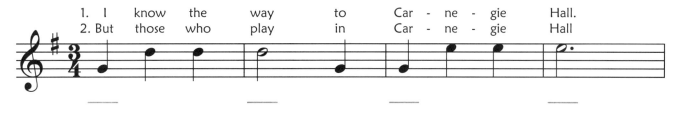

Encore Performance

*You've been invited back to Carnegie Hall! Join the list of great performers by writing **I**, **IV** or **V⁷** on the blank line for the correct LH chord in each measure. Then play and count aloud.*

Learning Link

Carnegie Hall *in New York City is one of the world's most famous concert halls. Andrew Carnegie, a millionaire, secured the land and the money for construction of the hall that began in 1890. Since its opening in 1891, countless numbers of performers, composers and even presidents have graced the stages of the Hall. Some of these performers are named in the example below.*

1. **Now Play This:** Play and count aloud.

2. **Now Hear This:** Circle the pattern that your teacher plays.*

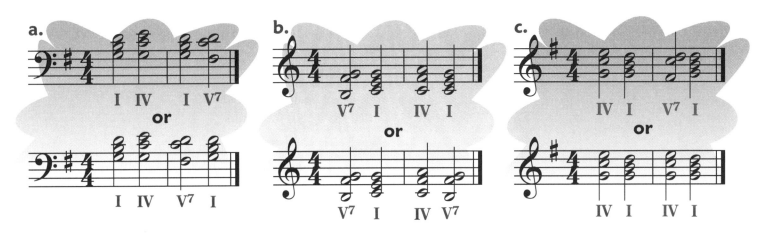

🪐 Imagination Station

*Create a chord pattern by writing **I**, **IV** or **V⁷** on each blank line.*
With your LH, play block chords in G, then C, using this rhythm.

*Note to Teacher:** Play one pattern from each exercise.

Fun Zone

What's Wrong with the MP3 Player?

The MP3 Player has downloaded the music incorrectly!
Check each example, decide what is wrong, then write
it correctly.

Learning Link

MP3 players are devices used
to download music from the
Internet. The players are smaller
than a personal CD player so they
are very portable. A computer is
needed to download music, and
the technology involved allows
users to store thousands of songs
onto the small MP3 player.

What's Wrong?	Fix It!
1. 𝄢 4/4 — I IV I	𝄢 4/4 — I IV I
2. G major key signature	G major key signature
3. 4/4 — Count: 1 2-3-4 5 1-2 3-4	4/4 — Count:
4. 𝄢♯ 4/4 — I IV I	𝄢♯ 4/4 — I IV I
5. *Allegro* = slow	*Allegro* = _____

Fun Zone All-State Band Festival

You have been invited to the All-State Band Festival.
Represent your school well by completing the rhythm examples.

1. Draw bar lines, then tap and count aloud.
Notice the time signature.

2. Write one note or rest in each measure, then tap
and count aloud. Notice the time signature.

3. Write one note in the empty box to equal the
total counts of the notes in the first box.

4. Circle the syncopated rhythm (**a** or **b**). Then tap both and count aloud.

Swing Style

1. In swing style,
   eighth notes are played:

long-short

short-long

(circle one)

Learning Link

Swing style *is a type of jazz music that became popular in the U. S. during the 1920s. Swing style jazz often includes the typical "long-short" eighth-note rhythm not usually notated in the music itself, but instead written as part of the tempo marking. Swing bands were usually larger than other jazz bands and often featured strong percussion (rhythm) sections.*

2. Clap each pattern 2 times each day. First, clap with even eighth notes. Then clap in swing style with *long-short* eighth notes.

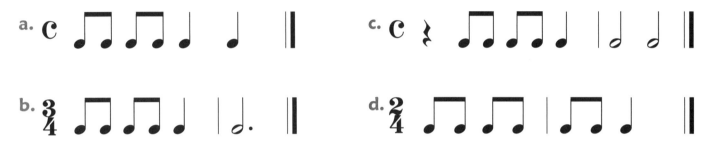

3. **Now Hear This:** Circle *swing style* or *even eighths* as you listen to your teacher clap each rhythm pattern.*

a. swing style
    even eighths

b. swing style
    even eighths

c. swing style
    even eighths

4. **Now Play This:** Play each example in swing style.

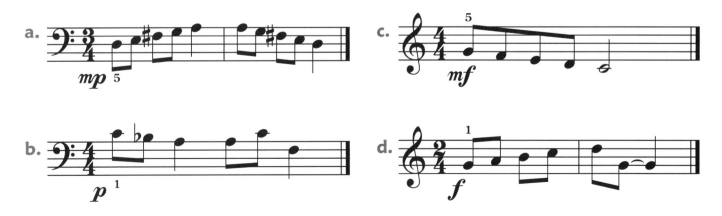

Note to Teacher: Clap each pattern either with *swing style* or *even eighths*.

Fun Zone   Singin' in the Rain

Notice the key signature and circle the letter name of the key above each umbrella. Then write the Roman numeral name of the chord (**I**, **IV** or **V⁷**) on the blank line.

Learning Link

The famous 1929 hit song, **Singin' in the Rain**, *is rated among the top 5 songs of the past 100 years. It has been recorded by many well-known singers. In 1952, dancer Gene Kelly directed and acted in one of the top musicals of all time, with the song serving as both the movie's title and its musical centerpiece. The film was nominated for an Academy Award for best music.*

(circle one)

1. Key of   **C**   **G**

2. Key of   **C**   **G**

3. Key of   **C**   **G**

4. Key of   **C**   **G**

5. Key of   **C**   **G**

6. Key of   **C**   **G**

7. Key of   **C**   **G**

8. Key of   **C**   **G**

F Major Scale

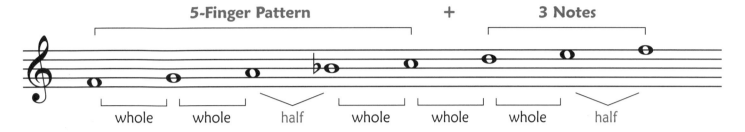

5-Finger Pattern + **3 Notes**

whole   whole   half   whole   whole   whole   half

1. Half steps occur between notes _____ – _____ and _____ – _____.

2. The flat in the F major scale is _____ ♭.

3. On the keyboard, write the letter names for the notes in the F major scale. Circle the keys that have a half step between them.

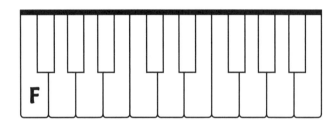

4. Using whole notes, write the F major scale going up. Circle the notes that have a half step between them.

5. On the blank lines above the notes, write the fingering for the RH F major scale. Then play.

6. On the blank lines below the notes, write the fingering for the LH F major scale. Then play.

1. **Now Hear This:** Your teacher will play an interval.*
Circle the interval that you hear.

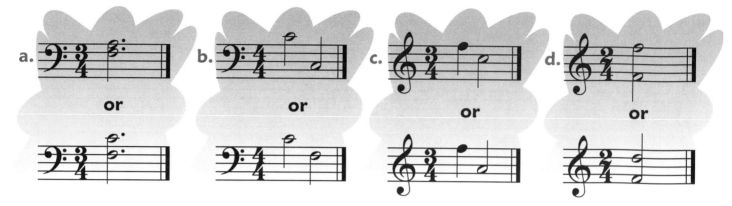

2. Name the key signatures:

a. Key of _____

b. Key of _____

c. Key of _____

This key has 1 flat.
Name the flat. _____

This key has 1 sharp.
Name the sharp. _____

3. Play this LH ending pattern.

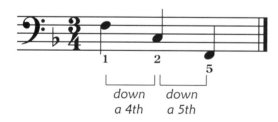

Learning Link

Leopold Mozart (1719–1787) was a composer, music teacher and violinist. He is best known as being the father and teacher of Wolfgang Amadeus Mozart. Although Leopold spent most of his time traveling throughout Europe with his gifted children, Wolfgang and Nannerl, his own compositions for keyboard are delightful and worthy of study. Enjoy performing the Leopold Mozart piece on page 21 of Lesson Book 3.

4. Write the LH ending pattern from example 3, beginning on C and then G. Then play each.

a.
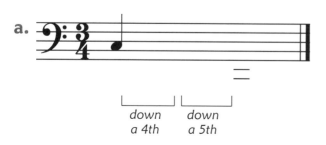

b.
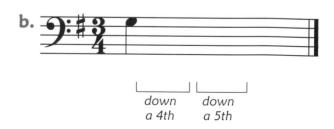

*Note to Teacher:** Play one interval from each exercise.

Primary Chords in F Major

1. Circle the Roman numerals that match the chord pattern on the staff.
   Then play the chords.

a.
      I V⁷ IV I

I V⁷ IV I
or
I IV V⁷ I

b.
IV V⁷ I
or
IV I V⁷

c.
V⁷   I
or
IV   I

2. Write **I, IV** or **V⁷** on each blank line. Then play and count aloud.

a.

mf

b.

mf

Imagination Station

*Historians have found the music for a minuet. Some LH measures
are incomplete. Review* Tips for Choosing the Correct Chord *on
page 7. Copy the correct chord (**a** or **b**) for each blank LH measure.
Then play and count aloud.*

a.

b.

The Lost Minuet

mf

5

16

1. **Now Hear This:** Circle the pattern that your teacher plays.*

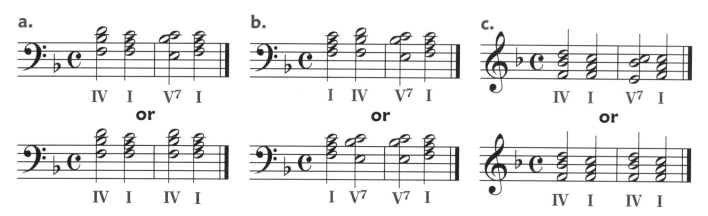

2. Using dotted half notes, write each waltz bass as a block chord in the second measure.
   Write the Roman numeral on the blank line. Then play.

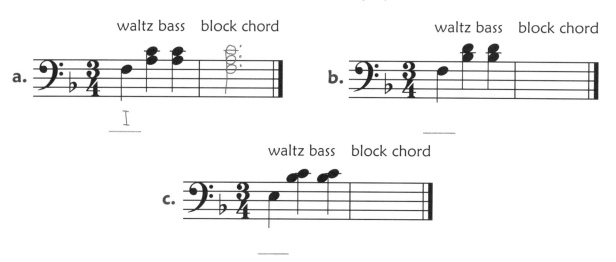

3. Using quarter notes, write each block chord as a waltz bass in the second measure.
   Write the Roman numeral on the blank line. Then play.

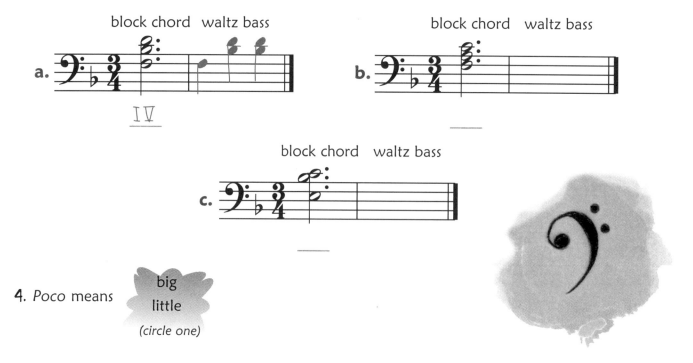

4. *Poco* means

big
little

(circle one)

Note to Teacher: Play one pattern from each exercise.

Bass Clef Ledger Lines

Below the Bass Staff

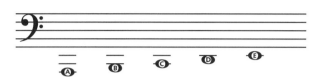

Above the Bass Staff

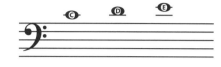

1. Write 2 notes that go up by 3rds. Use quarter notes. Name each note.

a.    b.

2. Draw a line to match each note to its keyboard.

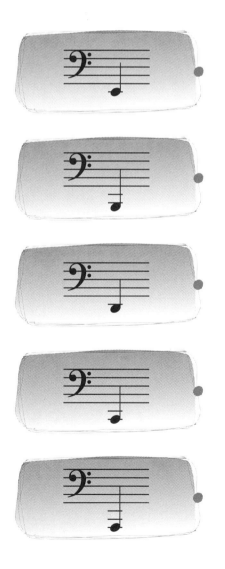

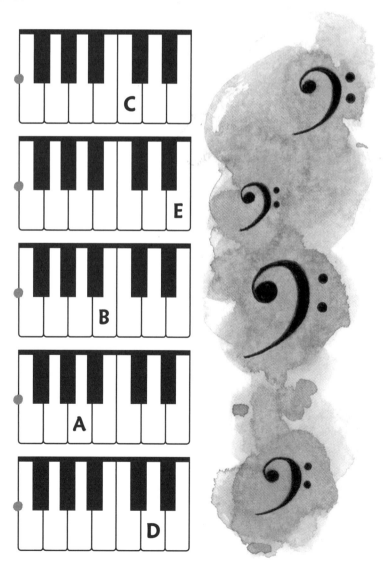

Lesson Book: page 27

Treble Clef Ledger Lines

Above the Treble Staff

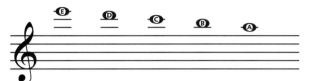

Below the Treble Staff

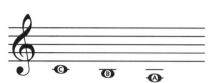

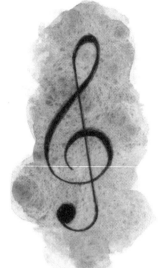

1. Write 2 notes that go up by 3rds. Use quarter notes. Name each note.

a.

b.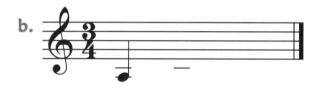

2. Write the name of each note on the blank line to spell a word.

a.

b.

c.

d.

3. Using a half note, write each melodic interval. Remember to add ledger lines.
Then write the name of each note on the blank line.

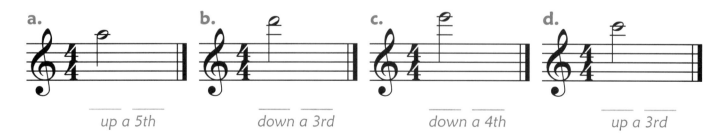

up a 5th   *down a 3rd*   *down a 4th*   *up a 3rd*

Fun Zone Test Pilot

Name and play each note as fast as you can. Time yourself and see how quickly you can complete this page. *Begin at the bottom of the page.*

Learning Link

The **sound barrier** is a term that applies to flying through space. It refers to a plane's transition of speed from subsonic (slower than the speed of sound) to supersonic (faster than the speed of sound).

The speed of sound varies depending on atmospheric conditions, with temperature being the most important. At sea level on a typical day, sound travels at speeds around 761 mph. At a height of 36,000 feet, a plane would have to fly faster than 660 mph to break through the sound barrier.

The speed of sound is referred to as Mach 1, named after Ernest Mach, a 19th century Austrian physicist.

8.

7.

6.

5.

4.

3.

2.

1.

Take off here.
Use any finger to play.

Rate Your Test Pilot Skills

_____ minute(s)

_____ seconds

Supersonic (less than 1 minute)
Mach 1 (1 minute)
Subsonic (more than 1 minute)

The Chromatic Scale

1. The chromatic scale is made up entirely of ▢ **half** / **whole** steps.

(circle one)

2. Starting with E, write the names of the notes on the keyboard to form a chromatic scale *going up*. Use sharps for black keys.

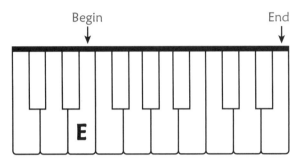

3. Starting with E, write the names of the notes on the keyboard to form a chromatic scale *going down*. Use flats for black keys.

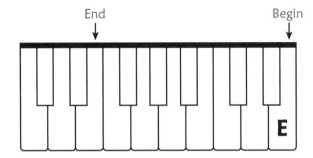

4. Write a sharp in front of the correct notes to form a chromatic scale *going up*.

5. Write a flat in front of the correct notes to form a chromatic scale *going down*.

6. *Molto* means ▢ **less, small** *or* **tiny** / **much, very** *or* **big**

(circle one)

Fun Zone Chromatic Autumn Colors

Draw a line to match the chromatic fingering pattern with its notes.

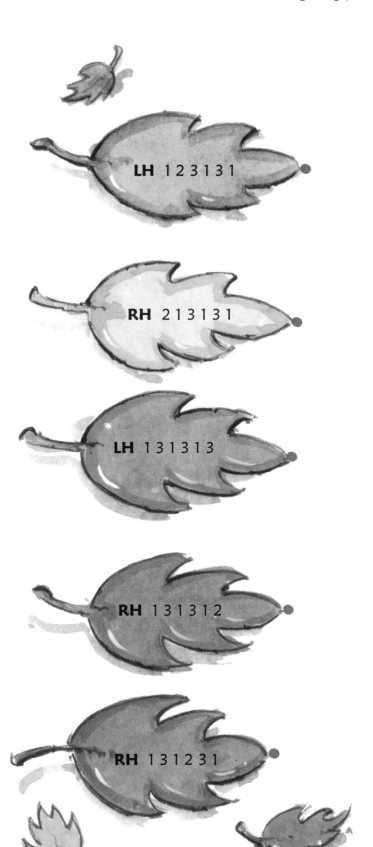

LH 1 2 3 1 3 1

RH 2 1 3 1 3 1

LH 1 3 1 3 1 3

RH 1 3 1 3 1 2

RH 1 3 1 2 3 1

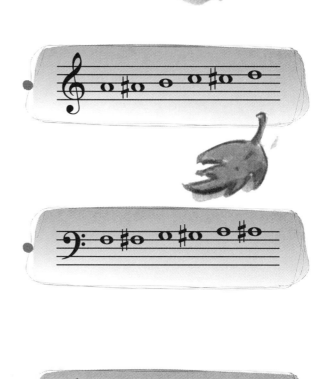

More About the Chromatic Scale

1. Finger  is used to play each black key
   in the chromatic scale.

                2
                3
(circle one)

2. Fingers
  1–2
  3–4
are used to play the white keys
   in the chromatic scale.
(circle one)

3. *Adagio* means
slowly
quickly
(circle one)

Learning Link

The **Painted Desert** in Arizona covers an area of 93,533 acres that stretches southeast from the Grand Canyon to the Petrified Forest National Park. The desert derives its name from the multicolored rocks that cover the park. Various combinations of minerals and decayed matter contribute to the many colors seen throughout the region.

4. On the blank lines above the notes, write the fingering
   for the RH chromatic scale *going up.* Then play.

5. On the blank lines below the notes, write the fingering
   for the LH chromatic scale *going down.* Then play.

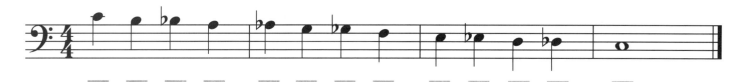

6. **Now Hear This:** Circle the pattern that your teacher plays.*

  a.   **b.**   **c.**

           or   **or**   **or**

*Note to Teacher: Play one pattern from each exercise.

$\frac{3}{8}$ Time Signature

1. Circle the correct answer for each statement below.

a. In $\frac{3}{8}$ time, there are 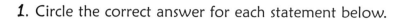 8 / 3 counts in every measure.

b. In $\frac{3}{8}$ time, the eighth note (♪) gets 1 / 3 count(s).

c. In $\frac{3}{8}$ time, the quarter note (♩) gets 1 / 2 count(s).

d. In $\frac{3}{8}$ time, the dotted quarter note (♩.) gets 2 / 3 count(s).

2. Draw bar lines in their correct places in the rhythm patterns below. Then tap with RH and count aloud.

3. Each rhythm example is missing a note. Choose the correct note and write it in the box. Then tap and count aloud.

Choose from:

More About $\frac{3}{8}$

1. Write **I**, **IV** or **V⁷** on the line. Then play and count aloud.

2. Now Hear This: Circle the rhythm that your teacher taps or claps.*

3. Write the correct time signature $\frac{3}{8}$ or $\frac{3}{4}$ before each example.
Then tap and count aloud.

☄Imagination Station

*Using this rhythm, create a RH melody with notes
chosen from the F major scale. Begin and end with F.*

*Note to Teacher: Tap or clap one pattern from each exercise.

$\frac{6}{8}$ Time

1. Circle the correct answer for each statement below.

   a. In $\frac{6}{8}$ time, there are counts in every measure.

   b. In $\frac{6}{8}$ time, the eighth note (♪) gets count.

   c. In $\frac{6}{8}$ time, the quarter note (♩) gets count(s).

   d. In $\frac{6}{8}$ time, the dotted quarter note (♩.) gets 1–1/2 / 3 count(s).

   e. In $\frac{6}{8}$ time, the dotted half note (♩.) gets 6 / 3 count(s).

2. Write the counts below each rhythm. Then tap and count aloud.

   a.

   1   2   3   4 – 5   6

   b.

3. Draw an X through one note or rest in each measure so that it has the correct number of counts.

   a.

   b.

4. Write the correct time signature **C** or $\frac{6}{8}$ before each example.
   Then tap and count aloud.

Lesson Book: page 37

Fun Zone

1. My Favorite Days of the Week

Write the counts below each rhythm. Then tap and count aloud each rhythm pattern.
Then tap and say the words.

"Sometimes on these days, you'll find me:"

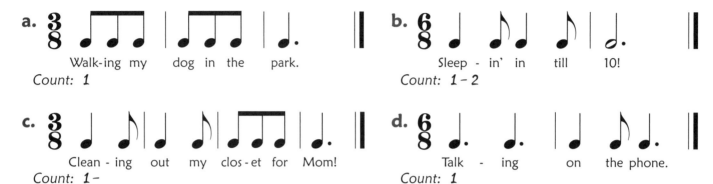

a. Walk-ing my dog in the park.
Count: 1

b. Sleep - in' in till 10!
Count: 1 - 2

c. Clean - ing out my clos-et for Mom!
Count: 1 -

d. Talk - ing on the phone.
Count: 1

What days could this be? _____ or _____

2. Play this LH pattern:

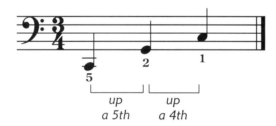

up a 5th   up a 4th

3. Write the LH pattern from example 2, beginning on F and then G. Then play each.

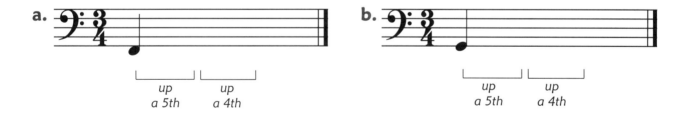

a. up a 5th   up a 4th

b. up a 5th   up a 4th

4. Cut 'n' Paste

Complete each rhythm example by choosing 1 note from the box,
then "pasting" it by drawing it in the example.

Choose from:

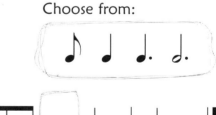

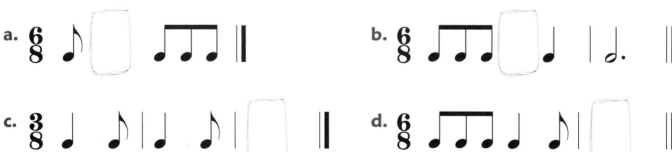

1. **Now Play This:** Play and count aloud.

a.

b.

c.

d.

Learning Link

*The **tarantella** is a traditional, southern Italian couples dance in $\frac{6}{8}$ time that gradually becomes faster and faster. The dancers are usually accompanied by mandolins, guitars and tambourines. The ancient tarantella legend says that the victims of the tarantula spider bite would frantically dance until they were cured. Although this legend creates the impression that tarantulas are dangerous spiders, they actually are very shy creatures.*

2. **Now Hear This:** Circle the rhythm that your teacher taps or claps.*

3. $\frac{6}{8}$ **Mind Twister**

In $\frac{6}{8}$ time, write 3 notes to equal the counts.

a. **3 counts =**

b. **6 counts =**

***Note to Teacher:** Tap or clap one pattern from each exercise.*

D Major Scale

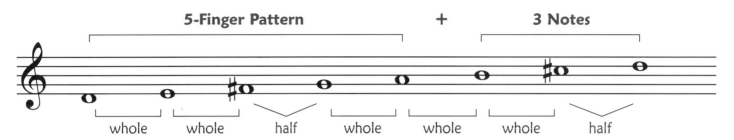

1. Half steps occur between notes _____ – _____ and _____ – _____ .

2. The sharps in the D major scale are _____ ♯ and _____ ♯ .

3. On the keyboard, write the letter names for the notes in the D major scale. Circle the keys that have a half step between them.

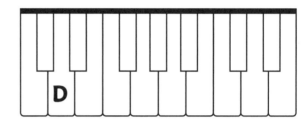

4. Using whole notes, write the D major scale going up. Circle the notes that have a half step between them.

5. On the blank lines above the notes, write the fingering for the RH D major scale. Then play.

6. On the blank lines below the notes, write the fingering for the LH D major scale. Then play.

Fun Zone **Photo Safari**

Complete each musical example as you travel on your African photo safari. *Begin at the bottom of the page.*

5. Complete the LH D major scale fingering.

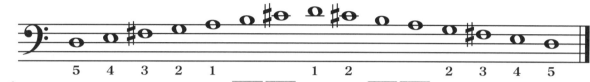

5   4   3   2   1   _____ _____ 1   2   _____ _____ 2   3   4   5

4. Write the D major key signature in treble clef.

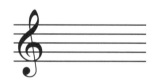

3. Complete the LH D major scale.

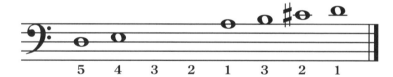

5   4   3   2   1   3   2   1

2. Write the D major key signature in bass clef.

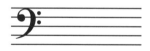

1. Complete the RH D major scale.

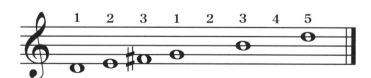

1   2   3   1   2   3   4   5

Begin Here

1. **Now Play This:** Play and count aloud.

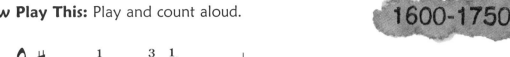

2. **Now Hear This:** Circle the pattern that your teacher plays.*

3. Using these rhythms, play **I**, **IV** and **V⁷** in D by reading the chord symbols.

Starting Chord

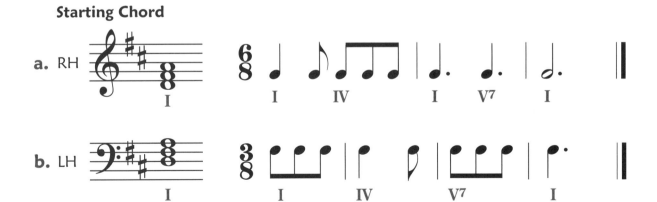

*Note to Teacher: Play one pattern from each exercise.

Fun Zone **Time Traveler**

Travel through time in the Music Imagination Machine.
Begin at the bottom of the page.

6. Clap and count aloud.

5. Name the chords (**I**, **IV** or **V⁷**). Then play.

4. *Adagio* means _____.

3. Play and count.

2. Name the notes. Then play.

1. *Poco* means
big
little
(circle one)

Begin here

Fun Zone Mr. Noteworthy's Review Quiz

The school music teacher, Mr. Noteworthy,
is preparing your class for the music festival.
Circle TRUE or FALSE for each example.
If *any part* of the example is not true, circle FALSE.

Symbol or Term	Name	Meaning	Circle One
1. ⌐1.⌐ :‖	1st ending	Play 2nd time only.	TRUE FALSE
2. D. C. al Coda	Da Capo al Coda	Go back 2 measures	TRUE FALSE
3. poco	Italian term	little	TRUE FALSE
4. 𝄢 (ledger-line note)	A	Ledger-line note below bass staff	TRUE FALSE
5. 𝄞 (ledger-line note)	B	Ledger-line note below treble staff	TRUE FALSE
6. 𝟛/𝟠	𝟛/𝟠 key signature	3 counts in every measure quarter note ♩ gets 1 count	TRUE FALSE
7. molto	Italian term	much, very *or* big	TRUE FALSE